The Fruit of the Spirit

EVIDENCE OF A FLOURISHING CHRISTIAN LIFE

I0895012

BEACON HILL PRESS
OF KANSAS CITY

The Fruit of the Spirit

EVIDENCE OF A FLOURISHING CHRISTIAN LIFE

Editor
Mike L. Wonch
Director of Curriculum
Merritt J. Nielson
Writers
Christina Bohn
C. Jeanne Orjala Serrão

King James Version (KJV)

ISBN: 978-0-8341-3100-2
Printed in U.S.A.

10 9 8 7 6 5 4 3 2 1

CONTENTS

Based on Galatians 5:22-23, this book is about living life by the fruit of the Spirit. It is designed to unpack each fruit or virtue on the list to help people understand them and how each aspect of the fruit of the Spirit can make a difference in their lives through the power of the Holy Spirit.

The great missionary apostle Paul was the author of the letter to the Galatian Christians who lived in what is now central Turkey. These people were a mixture of ethnicities and most came from pagan backgrounds. Paul wanted them to understand specifically that what they believed worked itself out in how they lived their lives. Paul grew up a first century Jew who understood that what a person really believed is revealed in how they act.

This was not the understanding of the Hellenized culture of the Galatians in the first century. They tended to think that the mind was separate from the body, so one could think one way, but act in another way. As Paul explains the fruit of the Spirit, he is using a metaphor to impress upon them that just as an apple tree produces apples, so Christians produce actions which reflect their Christ-like nature.

Pleasing God is all about living a life which reflects the work of His Holy Spirit in our lives—a life which exhibits the fruit of the Spirit, which this book is talking about. One caution, we are not living this life in our own strength! The fruit of the Spirit flow out of the Holy Spirit who lives within us.

Dr. C. Jeanne Orjala Serrão is the Dean of the School of Theology and Philosophy and Professor of Biblical Literature at Mount Vernon Nazarene University. She earned her BA in Biblical Literature from Mid-America Nazarene University, and an M.Div. and an M.A. in Missions from Nazarene Theological Seminary and her Ph.D. degree from Claremont Graduate University. She is an ordained elder in the Church of the Nazarene.

Christina Bohn is an instructor of Biblical Literature at Mount Vernon Nazarene University where she teaches Bible and Hebrew classes. In 2010, she completed a M.A. of Biblical Studies from Asbury Theological Seminary. She is heavily involved in ministries that welcome immigrants into the United States and aid them in adjusting to their new culture.

Love

Love in English is a rather vague word and can be used in reference to people, things or actions. I love my husband, I love chocolate and I love to knit. Obviously "love" doesn't mean the same thing in each case! So the context in which it is used, determines its meaning. Since Paul grew up a Jew who studied the Hebrew Bible or Old Testament, let's look first at the Hebrew view of love.

The Hebrew word for love, *ahav,* is used for everything from passionate, sexual love to the love of God for His people. The Old Testament confirms that love is the ultimate foundation of the covenant God made with His people, Israel. But when love is used in relation to God, the emotional aspect is generally de-emphasized—although there are a few times when it comes through. Love is the basic feeling of the religious in relation to God. Most of the time only groups of people are the objects of God's love. In Hosea we see a spontaneous side of God's love which binds Him to His people. In Isaiah we encounter the Father-God, or authoritarian love of God, and in Jeremiah we hear of the suffering love of God.

The Hebrew concept of love tends to emphasize inwardness and loyalty and rarely moved out of the borders of the people of God. Hillel, a rabbi in whose thoughts Paul was schooled, was one of those exceptions. He taught that in addition to the love for fellow Jews, one was to love all creatures and lead them to the law. Perhaps he was influenced by the universal love of Greek thought to which I will be turning shortly. But for the Jews of the first century, love was a relationship of faithfulness between God and humanity. It included love for God, but the source of this love was found in God. So the basic principle of love is a 3-fold relationship of God, a person and one's neighbor.

Jesus continued in the Hebrew tradition and gave us the two most important commandments: Love for God and love for neighbor. Up to this point, His Jewish friends would be with Him 100%; but Jesus goes on in several instances to show that His concept of neighbor was not limited to the community of Jews, but to anyone who needs help. We find this in the parable of the Good Samaritan, but also in Luke 4 where God's love extends to the Gentiles in Sidon and Syria. For Jesus, love is a matter of will and action. Love for God demands a readiness to do what He asks in an unconditional manner—it is a glowing passion for God!

Reflect on this...

Think about the various ways God loves His people. What does that tell us about the kind of love Paul is talking about here in Galatians, as a fruit of the Spirit of God?

If we use Jesus' expansive definition of "neighbor," who in your community would that refer to?

Paul continues in this tradition, adding the idea that the love of God is the love of Christ and that the Church is an indivisible fellowship with Christ at the center. He re-emphasizes that the love of God implies decision. God is the one who establishes the relationship and He is the one who gives us

the basic principle of love is a 3-fold relationship of God, a person and one's neighbor

His Spirit that produces love. So the work of love is God's goal from the beginning. The goal of God's love is salvation and the new creation.

In ancient Greece there were three words for love; *eros, philos* and *agapē*. *Eros* was by far the most important word for love in Greek literature and described the passionate love which desires the other for itself. In philosophy, from Plato on, *eros* is the epitome of uttermost fulfillment and elevation of life.

Eros, or ecstasy, was religion for these Gentiles. The mystery religions of the Greeks looked for an experience which set the senses in a frenzy, burst them out of their humanity and lifted a person above himself or herself. One scholar describes it as "All the forces of heaven and earth are second to the supreme power of *eros*. . . . No choice is left, nor will, nor freedom, to the [one] who is seized by its tyrannical omnipotence, and he [or she] finds supreme bliss in being mastered by it."[1]

The second word for love in Greek is *philos,* or the love of a friend for a friend. This connotes a warm human love between equals. It is not an impulse or "intoxication" that overcomes a person, but an act or task a person may choose to become involved in.

The last word for love, *agapē*, for the Greeks, had nothing of the power of *eros*, and little of the warmth of *philos*. It meant to be satisfied with something and indicated a choice or a preference. So if you loved (*agapaō*) someone or something, you preferred it to another person or thing. *Eros* is a general love of the world that seeks satisfaction wherever it can find it, *agapē* is a love that makes distinctions, chooses and is loyal to its love. *Eros* is impulsive, *agapē* is a "free and decisive act." *Eros* is characteristic of the Greek love of a person for the divine; while *agape* is descriptive of the condescending love of a god, which lifts the one of lower status. *Eros* seeks to fulfill its own desires while *agapē* is a giving love which acts on the behalf of others.[2]

So, if you were Paul, which Greek word would you use to convey the idea of Christian love? Paul, in the tradition of the Septuagint (the Greek translation of the Old Testament) chose the Greek word *agapē* and pours into it the particular meaning of Christian love—God's love for human beings, Christian love between fellow believers and the Christian's love for God.

The best place to see this is in 1 Corinthians 13. The first three verses of chapter 13 talk about the necessity of *agapē* love for those in the Church.

Reflect on this...

Think about the three Church audiences Paul is addressing in 1 Corinthians 13:1-3. Do these compare to modern audiences who need to understand the meaning of God's love?

Take time to read 1 Corinthians 13.

Love is kind. This is a rich word which means grace-filled, or gracious, compassionate service to another. It is also closely associated with the idea of being good citizen or person who is deeply appreciated in a community.

Love does not envy or boast and is not proud. It is easy to cry and pray with those who are having problems.

Love is not rude. How contrary to much of our culture this is! But it goes back to the idea that each person is a creation of God who deserves our respect. Christian love is not self-seeking; it is others-oriented.

Love is not easily angered and keeps no record of wrongs. Selfish people get irritated easily when people or things get in the way of their desires. Christian love looks out for the good of the other person and is patient when things don't go their way.

Love does not delight in evil but rejoices in the truth. Some scholars personify "the Truth" and see it as referring to Christ. However, I don't think it needs to be limited to that. Christian love will always be a force for the truth in whatever situation it finds itself in.

Love always protects. In other words, Christian love will not gossip or say things that will be hurtful to another's reputation. How difficult this is sometimes when there is a person or group of persons our associates love to make fun of or complain about! But Paul tells us that love always protects!

Love always trusts and always hopes. Sounds kind of naive to our modern ears! Love ALWAYS trusts and ALWAYS hopes? Come on—isn't there a point at which we stop trusting and hoping? As much as we may want to deny it, Christian love is optimistic and looks on the positive side of situations and issues.

Love always perseveres and never drops out. The Greek word is "falls" not "fail" and indicates that love outlasts everything. If there is one thing we need today it is Christians who will persevere and stay through the conflicts that inevitably come when there are groups of people living and working together.

Christian love, *agapē* as defined by Paul, is a unique love whose source is God. Let's ask God to give us His Spirit that will produce this love in our hearts! Then whatever our abilities, Christian love will make them effective for God's kingdom and fulfilling and rich experiences for us.

Reflection on this...

Which aspect of "agapē" is the most difficult for you? Why?

Ask God to remind you in the hurry of life, of the characteristics of His love and to give you the ability to act with "agapē" love.

NOTES

2

Joy

Have you ever met someone who is so full of joy it's contagious? Someone who is such a delight to be around that you find yourself naturally gravitating toward them? I once met a delivery worker in my neighborhood who had more joy than I had ever seen in one person before. You would think that delivering packages would get very monotonous after a while, but each day this man dropped off parcels with such enthusiasm that it was impossible not to notice. He greeted each person along his route and smiled and waved as he drove the large truck down the street. His joy was so contagious that I had to suppress the urge to cheer him on as he placed boxes on my neighbor's door.

It's difficult to find joy in the everydayness of life. Yet, in the words of C. S. Lewis, "joy is the serious business of heaven."[3] How "seriously" do we take joy? We expect ourselves as believers to adhere to certain doctrines, to avoid certain sins, to pray and read our Bibles regularly, but do we expect that we will gradually become more joyful? That we will become a source of "living water" to others? That we will be able to exhibit delight in the midst of the mundane? According to the Bible, joy is not an option. It is required of us. In other words, living a life characterized by joylessness is a sin.

Of course, not all of life is happy. There are broken hearts and crushed dreams. Yet, even these moments in our lives contain the possibility to be times characterized by joy. Each moment of every day is pregnant with joy; we just have to look for it and welcome it into our lives. Joy is an "attitude that chooses to delight in what God is doing in Christ, in oneself and in others."[4] Cultivating joy, then, is a spiritual discipline. This may sound odd, because we often think of a "discipline" as avoiding certain things. It is odd to think of a celebration as a "discipline." Yet, this fruit of the Spirit must be learned. With God's help, we can become joyful people.

Reflect on this...

Think of the last time you experienced a real sense of joy. What caused you to celebrate life?

What are some things today that often distract us from joy?

Where do you find joy in your current life situations?

In the Old Testament, joy is often connected with feasts. The Israelites observed several festivals that celebrated God's involvement in their history. It was a way that they expressed delight and gratitude for God's protection of them as a nation and for His ongoing presence among them. In fact, these feasts are often simply referred to as "times of rejoicing" (Numbers 10:10). One particularly joyous celebration was when the Israelites returned back to their land in Palestine and began rebuilding Jerusalem. When they read the Law at the foundation of the temple, their mourning was changed into rejoicing and they held a festival to commemorate this event (Nehemiah 8).

The Old Testament does not only describe human beings as exhibiting joy; it often describes God as being the subject who rejoices (Deuteronomy 30:9; Psalm 104:31; 147:11; 149:4; Zechariah 3:17). Joy is not just a human quality, but is an action that God himself does. However, imagine if God were not a genuinely joyful being. The miracle stories in the Gospels might read something like this:

It was 8:00 a.m. on a Monday and Jesus figured He might as well clock into work. He began teaching parables to the crowds, but He grew weary of it because He had just told the very same stories the previous day. The disciples then came to Him, explaining that the people had become very hungry while Jesus monotonously droned His way through one of His stories. Sighing heavily, Jesus muttered, "Tell them to find their own food. This is not part of my job description," and wearily trudged away. Along the road, a blind man came to Jesus and begged Him to heal his sight. Rolling His eyes, Jesus touched the man in passing, not even bothering to come to a halt. The man exclaimed, "Wait! I can see a little better, but everything looks blurry!" Jesus did not even look back at the man as He shouted, "20/70 vision is better than nothing." He then continued down the road, wallowing in His own self-pity.

Can you imagine if this was what Jesus had been like? Fortunately, this is not the kind of God we see in the Bible. In both the Old Testament and New Testament, God has a great desire to interact with humanity. Joy is written all throughout the creation account as God creates and then declares that it is "good." God did not mechanically create as part of a dismal routine, uninterested and impersonally involved. Rather, He found delight with His creations. At the end of the sixth day, God declared that everything He made was "exceedingly good." In the New Testament, we can only imagine Jesus' joy as He healed people of the infirmities they had had since they were born. In fact, over 40 references to joy and rejoicing occur in the Gospels.[5] Repeatedly in Scripture we see that God takes great delight in His people. Zephaniah 3:17 declares, "The Lord your God is with you, the Mighty Warrior who saves. He will take great delight in you; in his love he will no longer rebuke you, but will rejoice over you with singing."

Reflect on this...

Have you ever thought about God as a joyful being? What kind of picture did you have of God while growing up in your church or home?

Think of the ways that Scripture describes God's sense of joy. What do these instances say about the person of God?

For this reason, it is no wonder that joy in the Old Testament is used overwhelmingly to describe a spiritual state of the believer. Because God himself is overflowing with joy, joy is a natural product of life with God. Joy comes by simply being in the presence of God (1 Chronicles 16:27; Job 22:21-26; Psalm 9:2; 16:5-11). It is God's desire that we exhibit the same kind of joy that He possesses. After commanding His disciples to love one another, Jesus said, "I have told you this so that my joy may be in you and that your joy may be complete" (John 15:11). A way that God has given us access to His joy is through the ministry of the Holy Spirit. In the New Testament, joy is especially connected with the Holy Spirit's work in the believer's life. This is particularly evident in the book of Acts, where rejoicing and celebration occurs after the new believers are filled with the Holy Spirit (Acts 2:42-47; 8:37-39).

It is God's desire that we exhibit the same kind of joy that He possesses.

Elsewhere, many of the New Testament authors describe joy as a paradox. Joy is not only experienced during the good times in our lives, but it can be experienced in the midst of suffering (Matthew 5:11-12; Acts 5:41; 2 Corinthians 7:4; Colossians 1:24; 1 Thessalonians 1:6; James 1:2-3). Even though this world is fallen and circumstances may be outside of our control, we can still live a life characterized by God's enduring joy. An example of this is seen when Paul and Silas were beaten and placed in a Philippian prison. In the midst of this persecution, they both worshipped God through song (Acts 16:25).

One of the reasons we can exhibit joy in the midst of suffering is because we know that this life is not the final end. Human history will culminate in one grand event, where the Groom will return for His bride (Revelation 19:7). This wedding will mark the beginning of a never-ending celebration.

This final installation of permanent joy is the means by which we can learn to approach life with the hopeful expectation that God can bring joy to us today. "This is the day which the Lord has made," the psalmist writes. "I will rejoice and be glad in it" (Psalm 118:24). We can think about how happy we were yesterday or speculate about how happy we may be in the future, but in reality today is all we have. Let's welcome it and find something to be joyful about.

Reflect on this...

Consider setting time aside to celebrate what God has done in your life. Do the activities you enjoy, gather with others who are joyful and eat the foods you love. Welcome God to take part of your celebration.

NOTES:

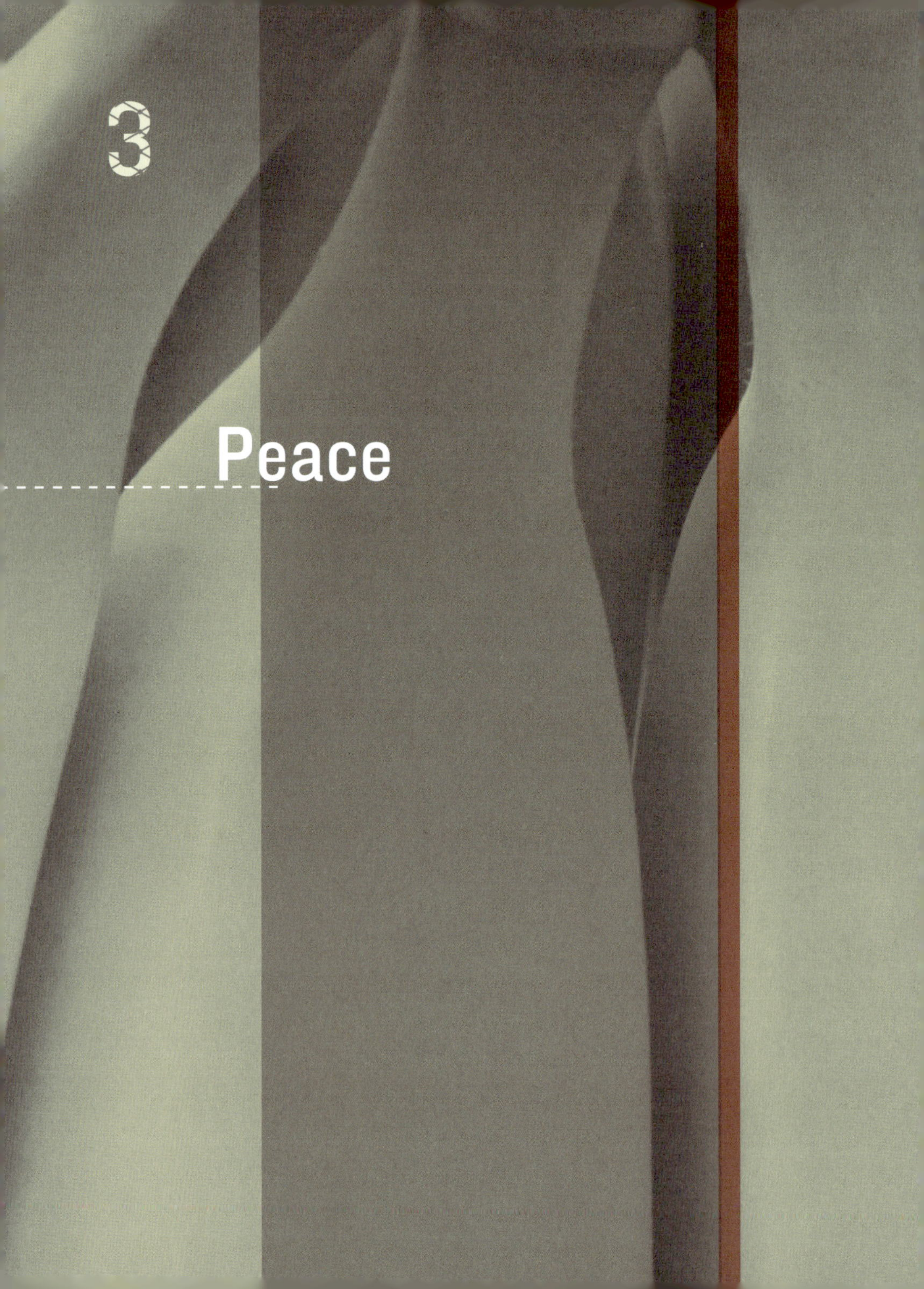

3

Peace

Once, when I served as a youth pastor, I taught a lesson to the middle school students about peace. We discussed what God's peace looked like and how we could implement it into the world. We imagined what the world would look like when there would be perfect peace. I was just about to finish the lesson, confident that it had been a success, when one of the middle-school boys interrupted me.

"I don't think that a world with peace would be very much fun," he contended.

Puzzled, I asked him why he thought this way.

"If there wasn't any violence or killing," he replied, "there wouldn't be any good movies or video games."

I tried to wipe my face of shock. Several of the students nodded their heads in agreement. This lesson had not gone in a way I had anticipated!

With a world saturated with violence, it is very difficult for us to imagine an alternative. Peace seems impossible, sometimes even unattractive, to our human nature. We often read Jesus' words of "turning the other cheek" and Paul's admonition to "repay evil with good" and assume that these are merely suggestions. Perfect peace is too idealistic for our fallen world. Yet, Paul included peace as one of the first items in his list of the fruit of the Spirit. Just like Paul, we need to imagine another way. We need to dare to think that not only is another way possible, but it is commanded of us. What is the biblical definition of peace and how do we live "peace" out in our lives?

In Greek thought, *eirēnē* (the Greek word for peace) primarily consisted of the absence of war or conflict. It denoted a specific state, not so much an attitude or relationship. This ideology is especially demonstrated in the *pax Romana*, when the Roman Empire had attained legal "peace" or security. Although a Roman citizen, it appears that Paul primarily gathered his understanding of peace from his Jewish heritage. Paul undoubtedly appreciated the *pax Romana*, but his ministry was inspired by the *pax Christi* (peace of Christ).

Reflect on this...

What are some images that appear when you first think of "peace?" How do you react to them?

Why do you think that peace seems so idealistic in our society today?

The Hebrew word *shalom* informs the Christian understanding of peace in the New Testament. It has a sense of totality or wholeness behind it and often refers to restoring something to the way it was intended, so that the end result is "complete." Thus, peace is not merely the absence of war or disaster; it is the presence of something. We typically only talk about "peace" as the void of conflict and turmoil. However, a city without political conflict is not true peace according to the biblical definition. For a city to experience real peace there must be friendly relations with the "enemy."

Peace is not merely the absence of war or disaster; it is the presence of something.

Interestingly, the Old Testament never uses peace to refer to an inner state of tranquility, like we typically think of it in the Western world. The most common use of *shalom* in the Old Testament is in reference to an external material or physical state. For example, when David went to check on his brothers at the battlefield, he asked if they had "peace." In other words, David wanted to know if they were physically healthy and safe. Most English Bibles translate *shalom* in such a way as "well," so we often overlook this biblical concept of peace. *Shalom* is also used to refer to the physical state of circumstances. How is the situation? Are things as they should be? (2 Kings 5:21, 22; 9:11) Many times, *shalom* does not indicate that a situation is just "okay." Rather, it indicates that there is prosperity or abundance. When there is peace, people are not just "getting along" or "making it," but they are flourishing. Pairing peace with prosperity is very characteristic of the prophetic writings, especially when they paint a picture of Israel's future hope (see Jeremiah 33:6, 9; Malachi 2:5).

Based on this biblical meaning, peace should be understood by the presence of material welfare along with the absence of physical danger. Once again, it must be stressed that *shalom* is the positive presence of something. When there is true peace, things are the way that God intended for them to be. Peace does not simply avoid strife; peace strives to bring wholeness to others, including material well-being. The former (no war) is passive peacekeeping, while the latter (wholeness) is active peacemaking.

The second most dominant use of *shalom* in the Old Testament is linked to justice. This is illustrated by the many times that peace is paralleled with righteousness and justice. When God's justice is done, the result is *shalom*. In other words, peace does not just happen on its own; it must be pursued by God's people. Over and over again, the prophets criticized Israel for not pursuing justice. Instead, they oppressed others, resulting in the very opposite of peace (Amos 5:4-15; 21-24; Jeremiah 7:1-20; 22:1-15). The prophets also repeatedly talked about *shalom* as a future hope when God would judge the earth and instill His righteousness (Isaiah 9:1-7; 11:1-9; 60:15-22; Jeremiah 23:5-6). Just like the prophets, we eagerly await God's help in making this world "right" and establishing His peace through His kingdom reign.

In the New Testament, Paul roots his understanding of peace in his Old Testament background. In many of his letters to both churches and individuals he greets his recipients by wishing them "peace." In Romans 12:18 and 14:17-19 Paul urges the Roman believers to live at peace with everyone. Again in 2 Corinthians 13 Paul writes, "Strive for full restoration, encourage one another, be of one mind, live in peace" (v. 11). Apparently, Paul saw peace as the mark of followers of Christ. Since God has brought reconciliation to us through Jesus Christ, so we too are to strive for reconciliation with others. Consistent with the Old Testament, this kind of reconciliation is of the whole person. As Paul writes, "the mind governed by the Spirit is life and peace" (Romans 8:6). Peace is a God's gift to people who live faithfully within his covenant.[6]

Reflect on this...

How does peace as a person's overall wellness differ from how we discuss peace today? How is it consistent?

How would you define "justice?" What are some parallels that you see between justice/righteousness and peace?

Application

Today when we typically ask God for "peace" we are requesting some sort of emotional state. We want an internal state of stillness and calm. Although this is one part of peace, this does not fully encapsulate all that peace really entails. As we saw in the Old Testament usage, *shalom* is used to denote a full sense of wholeness. This wholeness is both physical and relational, true to the overall intentions that God has for this world. Instead of desiring an inward state of peace or even the absence of conflict in our lives, we as Christians should be bearing this fruit by passionately bringing true peace into our circle of influence.

Seeking peace is not an optional practice for Christians. It is not something too idealistic that cannot be implemented into this world until Christ returns. When Jesus listed peacemaking as a practice of the new Christian community, He was not giving us a suggestion; He was giving us a command (Matthew 5:9). Notice that Christ does not command us to be "peace-keepers," but to actively "make peace."

Sometimes it may seem like we are playing in an idealistic make-believe land that seems completely out of reach when compared to this seemingly hopeless state of the world. But, as Frederick Buechner writes, "maybe what is good about religion is playing that the kingdom will come, until—in the joy of your playing, the hope and rhythm and comradeship and poignance and mystery of it—you start to see that playing is itself the first-fruits of the kingdom's coming and of God's presence within us and among us."[7] Although we may not be able to make perfect peace evident on this war-torn earth, we as the Church can nevertheless plow and prepare places for God to make true peace implanted through His kingdom reign.

Reflect on this...

Identify some areas in your own life that are not whole. What would it look like for shalom to be present?

When peace seems out of our control as human beings, we need to pray for God to work within our situations. Think of praying for peace as a part of bearing the "fruit of the Spirit."

NOTES:

4

Patience (Forbearance) and Goodness

Patience and goodness are two more virtues describing the fruit of the Spirit which are also associated with characteristics of God. Down through the centuries human beings have struggled with being patient, how long to be patient and with whom to be patient. Scholars and theologians have argued over whether a human being can be "good" or not, but certainly everyone hopes that their neighbor is good. Goodness and patience are two characteristics we hope our supervisor has and which we often lament as characteristics we would like to see more of in our own lives.

In ancient Greek, patience (*makrothymia*) carried a rather negative meaning (for us) of "resignation" or "forced acceptance."[8] In this context it was tied closely to their understanding that human beings' lives are controlled by fate and therefore the only thing one can do is adjust one's attitude toward what is happening. So the persons who resigned to their fate were actually wise people who stopped kicking against the inevitable and began accepting their destiny and learning to live with it. We might relate to this more if we use the word "endurance."

We don't believe in fate, but certainly in our experience there are times when we have to endure difficult times. We have to learn to be patience with how things are for the present as we wait for God's direction and opportunities for improvement or change. For some of us, patience with sickness, either our own or of a family member, is difficult. We can either choose to be impatient and stress-out about the situation, or we can learn to be patient, do what is necessary to bring healing and wholeness to the situation and be a positive influence.

In the Old Testament and Jewish tradition peace is strongly associated with the nature of God. God is patient with His people who seem to continually forget God, break their covenant and worship other gods. It is God's patience which saves human beings from God's wrath and their total destruction. But God's patience with us requires that we be patient with others (Jeremiah 15:15), especially those we have power over (Proverbs 14:28-29). In the Old Testament, God's patience is seen as a gift from God (Psalms 86:15-17). Through patience, God extends grace to His people, sparing them from deserved wrath and giving them time to repent and return to the promises they have made (see Exodus 34:6-7).

Reflect on this...

Have you experienced God's patience with you? If so, how were you made aware of His patience? If not, how would you know if He was patient with you?

Why do you think God expects us to be patient with others when He is patient with us?

For Paul, patience is important to the unity of the Church. In Ephesians 4:2-3, he encourages the Christians to be patient with each other, "bearing with one another in love." The nature of love, as Paul sees it, is to have patience and with patience we can joyfully endure whatever comes—both as individuals and as a community. Sometimes we Christians are careful to be patient with co-workers or non-Christians, but we lose that patience with fellow brothers and sisters in Christ. Paul recognizes that patience is a key virtue for the Church to be unified in its mission and ministry

Patience is a key virtue for the Church to be unified in its mission and ministry.

Paul's letters and the General Epistles (letters) have to address the issues of heresy and the expectation of the return of Christ, growing concerns of the developing Church. Both of these issues require patience. James closes his letter encouraging his fellow Christians to bring back the brother or sister who wanders from the truth (James 5:19) so that they might be saved from death and "cover over a multitude of sins" (v. 20). Both of these reasons reveal that the desire to correct a fellow Christian comes from a love for that person, not a desire to show who is right and who is wrong. Paul, in his final instructions in 1 Thessalonians 5:14, indicates that the best way to correct those in the community is by being patient.

Reflect on this...

Why is it that we often are more patient with non-Christians than with our brothers and sisters in Christ?

What are some ways we can show patience and still correct or guide fellow Christians?

The virtue of "goodness" (*agathōsunē*) or generosity "is essentially synonymous with" kindness[9], which we will be looking at in the next chapter. Paul uses this noun in the New Testament, but its adjective, "good" is used over 100 times. Jesus claims that "No one is good—except God alone" (Mark 10:18 and Luke 18:19; see also, Matthew 19:17). This point makes the case again that those who are truly good can only be so because the Spirit of God is working through them.

Paul spends time talking about the meaning of goodness because it is a word that could be misunderstood by his Gentile readers. In Greek philosophy "goodness" is "what gives meaning" and is closely related to reason.[10] People can learn to be "good" through proper instruction and this was the role of philosophy. During the Hellenistic period, good came to be associated with salvation and doing what is pleasing to God or the gods.

Jesus and Paul echo the understanding of goodness found in the Old Testament. God is good and God's people come to understand what good is through God's revelation, specifically, the Law. Those who do good are good, but the Old Testament is not clear on whether it is possible for a human being to do good without God in their lives. Goodness is often associated with God's love. Psalm 25:7 says, "Remember not the sins of my youth and my rebellious ways; according to your love remember me, for you are good, O Lord." In Micah 6:8, God shows human beings what good is and that it is what God requires of us, "To act justly and to love mercy and to walk humbly with your God." Just from these two verses we can see that goodness has a broad meaning which comes directly from God's love for His creation and specifically for human beings. God's goodness is then reflected in His people who help to create a just society, are merciful to others and recognize their relationship to God.

In Romans 15:14, Paul tells his readers that he is convinced that they "are full of goodness." The rest of the passage continues to talk about things being "through the power of the Spirit" (v. 19). The context indicates that Paul is convinced of their goodness because of the Holy Spirit working through them. 2 Thessalonians 1:11 is similar in that Paul says "by his [God's] power he may fulfill every good purpose [goodness] of yours." Goodness is something Christians exhibit because the power of God is working through them.

Ephesians 5 begins with "Be imitators of God, therefore, as dearly loved children and live a life of love . . ." (5:1). Paul continues with contrasting the lifestyle of the world and the lifestyle of God's holy people. Then in verse 8, he introduces the contrast of light and darkness and in verse 9 lists the fruit of the light as "goodness, righteousness and truth." Darkness is "fruitless" and the Christian is to have nothing to do with the "deeds of darkness" (v. 11).

Using slightly different language, Ephesians confirms that the fruit of goodness comes as a result of trying to imitate God in living a life of love. And as John says "if we walk in the light as he is in the light, we have fellowship with one another, and the blood of Jesus, his Son, purifies us from all sin" (1 John 1:7). These verses clearly indicate that the fruitful Christian is one who lives in communion with God. They also point out that there is a level of personal will expressed in trying to be imitators of God by living a life of love and avoiding the activities associated with "darkness" or characteristic of those who do not live in communion with God.

Paul affirms his expectation and hope in Philippians 1:6: "Being confident of this, that he who began a good work in you will carry it on to completion until the day of Christ Jesus." The fruit of goodness is found in the persons who live in the light, live a life of love and allow God to work through them in the power of the Spirit. So it may be true, as Jesus said, that no one is good except God, but as the Christian seeks to imitate God, live in His presence, and do the acts of love which God's Holy Spirit prompts, goodness is produced in the Christian's life. ●

Reflect on this...

In what ways will you incorporate patience into your life this week?

In what ways will you incorporate goodness into your life this week?

NOTES:

5

Kindness and Gentleness

Kindness and gentleness are two very similar words, but Paul includes both of them in his list of the fruit of the Spirit. Perhaps Paul included both to emphasize the need for kindness and gentleness in the Greco-Roman "challenge culture" of the first century.[11] In this context, the person of slightly lower status was constantly challenging the person of higher status, trying to get society to acknowledge his worth and grant him more status. So in the first century setting, kindness or gentleness (meekness) could be seen as a sign of weakness. This is another clear indication that Jesus' message and Paul's gospel had turned the culture of the first century on its head as far as what was valued and emphasized.

The Septuagint (Greek version of the Old Testament) uses *chrēstotēs* (kindness) to translate Hebrew terms which mean "excellent," "genuine" or "costly."[12] When referring to people it means "serviceable," "good," or "useful."[13] The Old Testament sees the all-powerful God as also one who comes down to help His people, so we find *chrēstotēs* used in describing God and His actions (Psalms 34:8; 25:8; 52:9; 69:16; 106:1; Jerermiah 33:11). This would indicate that kindness is a characteristic of someone who has power, but choses to grant mercy even when it is not deserved. Even though God is portrayed as giving out stern judgment and punishment, it is based on the law which understands God as good and kind; "his ordinances are good" (Psalms 119:41; cf 65ff). We also observe that in Jewish tradition the word is used in the worship and praise of God.[14]

Reflect on this...

What stands out to you as a different meaning for kindness then what we usually attribute to this word? Is this significant? Why or why not?

If we keep in mind the idea that kindness is an important characteristic for the powerful, how does this affect our understanding of Ephesians 4:32 and Galatians 5:22-23?

In Galatians 5:22-23, where we find the list of the fruit of the Spirit, this Greek word is found in its noun form and is translated "gentleness" (KJV) or "kindness" (NIV). Out of the eight times the noun occurs in the New Testament, four are used to describe God, three in lists similar to our fruit of the Spirit list and once in Romans 3:12, a quotation of Psalm 53:3. All occurrences of this noun are found in the apostle Paul's writings.

Outside of Paul's writings, we find that Jesus used the adjective of this word in Matthew 11:30, "my yoke is *easy*," in Luke 5:39, referring to wine, "the old is *better*," and in Luke 6:35, referring to God, "he is *kind* to the ungrateful." 1 Peter 2:3 uses it in reference to the Lord, "now that you have tasted that the Lord is *good*" (*gracious* in KJV).

As you can see *chrēstotēs* is translated by several different English words: kindness, gentleness, or goodness for the noun and easy, better, kind, good, or gracious when it is describing someone or something. A Greek lexicon (dictionary) gives "goodness or uprightness" as its first definition and in reference to human beings and God, "goodness, kindness, and generosity."[15]

When we broaden our search for the use of this word by the ancient Greeks, we find it defined as: excellent, serviceable, useful, worthy, friendly, decent, honest, upright in a moral sense, and adapted to its purpose. This is similar to the Jewish use of the word except that it is not used in deity worship. The opposite of *chrēstotēs* in this literature is wicked or rough and surly.

So what can we conclude about this important word? From the Jewish and Christian use of this word, we must conclude that *kindness* is a characteristic of God. To the extent that God is imitated, Christians can also be *kind.* The ancient Greek definition, "adapted to its purpose," indicates that when we are *kind* we are being what we were created to be. Therefore, the Holy Spirit enables us to be what God created us to be: kind, good, morally upright, generous, friendly, or in short, *chrēstotēs.*

To the extent that God is imitated, Christians can also be kind.

Reflect on this...

Do you think that kindness as understood by Paul is valued by our present society? Why or why not?

Now that you understand the breadth of meaning for kindness, why do you think Paul wanted to emphasize it in the early churches?

How would the practice of kindness change our society? Our churches? Our families?

A close synonym for *chrēstotēs* is *praytēs* (gentleness). The question is, why would Paul use both these words, isn't kindness enough? Although these two words appear very close in English and are even translated by the same English words at times, there are some very significant differences between the two for Paul and his readers which we need to think about.

In the non-biblical Greek writings *praytēs* (gentleness) was used to indicate things that were mild (mild curry versus hot curry), tame or domesticated animals, gentle, quiet or pleasant people, and merciful punishments. It was valued as a manly virtue as long as it was balanced with strength and it indicated that the powerful man was also wise and cultured. It was highlighted especially as a virtue in women since the prevailing cultural view was that women should be quiet, gentle and pleasant. For women, it did not need to be balanced with strength, since weakness was the ancient characteristic description of women in contrast to men. For the Greek philosopher Aristotle it was the middle between bad temper and spineless incompetence, between extreme anger and indifference.[16] For the Greek philosophers, balance in temperament was the ideal and the wise person trained himself to become balanced.

In the Jewish literature, gentleness was appropriate for the position of a servant and so humble is a good way to translate the word. It is never used of God in the Old Testament, but was used to describe Moses as the humble servant of the Almighty God. The Old Testament writers indicate that gentleness in human beings is pleasing to God, an antidote to pride and arrogance and is the proper virtue for women. They also encourage the gentle to become warriors when needed, but gentleness was also a quality of a royal hero. Gentleness or humbleness was also seen in those who quietly bore suffering as what was required as a child of God.[17]

In the New Testament *gentleness* is seen in Jesus, but is always balanced by authority or love. Jesus calls himself *gentle* only in Matthew, the gospel where He is portrayed as the promised Messiah King. Here Jesus' authority or power is readily understood. In Corinthians Paul tells his readers that the gentleness of Christ is based in love and is not a sign of weakness. This is significant in Corinthians because it was written to a relatively young city where families were vying for status and *gentleness* would not have been a cherished virtue, especially if seen as a sign of weakness.

As far as the role of gentleness in the people of God, the Sermon on the Mount (Matthew 5:5) tells us that the meek (uses *praeis, adj. of praytēs*) will inherit the earth, indicating that they will rule with God in the end times. As we have seen in Paul it is a gift of the Spirit which enables us to correct our fellow Christians without pride or arrogance because we recognize our humble situation. In Peter's writings Christians are cautioned to defend their faith with *praytēs* and fear (1 Peter 3:5-6). Peter's readers are experiencing persecution, so Peter encourages them to give "the reason for the hope" they have in a way that will not antagonize their persecutors or increase the Christian's suffering needlessly.

In James 1:21 and 3:13 we find our word directly linked with how one accepts the gospel (word) and to how the wise and knowledgeable person communicates wisdom to the community. James reminds his primarily Jewish Christian readers that even though they have been taught the Torah since they were children, they must receive the gospel which saves them with humility. They must also share their wisdom and insights with humbleness to the rest of the church who may not have had the same opportunities. This section is followed by a description of divine wisdom which uses yet another word for gentleness (*epieikēs*) which emphasizes patience, especially in the context of anger, bitterness and contention.

Reflect on this...

Why do you think Paul wanted to emphasize gentleness or meekness in the early churches?

Do you think gentleness or meekness has an important role in our society? Do you see any dangers in over-emphasizing meekness or gentleness? Why or why not?

NOTES:

6

Faithfulness

It's early Saturday morning. Instead of sleeping in your warm, cozy bed, you are outside jogging in the early morning light. At first, it's invigorating. You feel especially motivated today to get your body back into shape. Your lungs breathe in the cool air, your muscles feel loose, the birds are chirping cheerfully. You feel at "one with the cosmos." Gradually, though, your feet start feeling like bricks. Your lungs start to burn as you wheeze heavily and soon a sharp cramp wedges itself into your calf muscle. You've reached the point that runners deem as "hitting the wall." At this stage, the temptation to stop is overwhelming. You're frustrated, because you've been running for days but can't seem to lengthen your running distance. You doubt whether all of this effort is even worth it. You'd rather be doing your couch-sitting, television-watching routine on Saturdays instead of subjecting your body to such agony.

Beginning the race is fun. The difficult part is finishing it. Anyone can begin a marathon, but only a few can actually cross the finish line. How will we run our life of faith? Will we remain faithful and finish well? Or when the road becomes difficult will we quit, crawling back into our safe bed, laying our crosses back down? In the book of Hebrews, the author writes, "Let us throw off everything that hinders and the sin that so easily entangles, and let us run with perseverance the race marked out for us" (12:1). In other words, we as believers must strive to remain faithful to God, even in the midst of opposition. Conversely, "everything that does not come from faith is sin" (Romans 14:23). But when Paul urges the church in Galatians to practice faithfulness as part of the fruit of the Spirit, what does that look like lived out in our lives?

Reflect on this...

When was a time when you "hit a wall" in your walk with God? How were you able to keep going?

What are some conditions in your life that make it very tempting for you to quit (such as stress, tiredness, strained relationships, and so on)?

In the Hebrew world, faith was the primary human reaction to a relationship with God. Since God was the one to whom every creature owed their existence, it was their duty to acknowledge Him as God. This sort of recognition was based on objectivity, not subjectivity.[18] In other words, it did not matter how a person felt or thought about the matter. He may not desire to place his faith in God, but the bottom line was that God deserved his faith. Because God is worthy of faith, it is the subject's obligation to believe. This was very different from the Greek's understanding of "faith," where the decision was based on intellect.

When a person was faithful to God, it was expected that she would have a moral response. Faith was not a set of ideas or theological propositions to believe about God; rather, it was a response of obedience. If you had faith in God, you would do what He required. Once again, this was a matter of the will, not a matter of the emotional feelings or intellect. This is a bit odd to us today, because we do not often think of faith as being a responsibility. For the

Israelites, on the other hand, obedience was the requirement that came with the "fear" (respectful awe, humility) of the Lord. For the Israelites, you either feared and obeyed, or you did neither. There was no in-between.

For the people of Israel, faithfulness was especially carried out by observing the covenant that God had made with them. The covenant required a mutuality of obligation, both on the part of God and Israel. All throughout Scripture, God remained faithful to His promises. Because He is a faithful God, "keeping his covenant of love to a thousand generations," it was Israel's responsibility to loyally uphold their terms of their covenantal agreement (Deuteronomy 7:9-11).

Reflect on this...

It is difficult to have faith when our emotions or intellect say something contrary. When was a time when you had to trust God instead of relying on your own intuition?

"Trust and obey, for there's no other way to be happy in Jesus . . ." goes the old hymn. How are trust and obedience related? How might they seem at odds?

The Bible has many examples of people who exhibited this type of faith and trust in God. Abraham is a paradigm of a person who demonstrated strong faithfulness. Time after time, God "tested" Abraham's faith and he in turn proved loyal. God gave Abraham instructions, and Abraham was expected to obey. Despite the seemingly impossible promises of God, Abraham "believed the Lord, and [God] credited it to him as righteousness" (Genesis 15:6). When God fulfilled His promise of giving Abraham a son, Isaac, God once again challenged Abraham. "Take your son, your only son, Isaac, whom you love, and go to the region of Moriah," God commanded. "Sacrifice him there as a burnt offering on one of the mountains I will tell you about" (Genesis 22:2). This demanded tenacious obedience on Abraham's part. Isaac was not just Abraham's son, but he was the fulfillment of God's promise.

As is exemplified in Abraham's story, faith is often not doubt-free certainty. As we look at Abraham's life, there were several instances when he and his wife Sarah had their doubts. Often we think of doubt as the opposite of faith, but sometimes doubt co-exists with faith. As Madeleine L'Engle writes, ""Those who believe they believe in God but without passion in the heart, without anguish of mind, without uncertainty, without doubt, and even at times without despair, believe only in the idea of God, and not in God himself."[19] Instead of being doubt-free, faithfulness is resolute obedience, even when God does not make sense.

However, it is important to notice that Abraham was not holding on to some type of "blind faith." This was not the first time that God had revealed himself to Abraham, nor was it the first time that God would prove His faithfulness. God had previously proved His faithfulness by giving Abraham the land He had promised. He was faithful to Abraham by miraculously giving him a son. Abraham had a relationship with God prior to this event, and it is upon these experiences that Abraham based his trust.

In the New Testament, the writer of Hebrews lists a large collection of people who like Abraham, demonstrated faith by their obedience. Even though these men and women did not have visible evidence that God would uphold His promises, they nevertheless trusted God. In other words, they demonstrated that "faith is being sure of what we hope for and certain of what we do not see" (Hebrews 11:1). By far, our most outstanding example of faithfulness is seen in the person of Jesus, who is the author and perfecter of our faith (Hebrews 12:2). Like Abraham, Jesus trusted God as He carried His cross down the lonely road that led to the "mountain" where He would be sacrificed. Like Abraham, Jesus desired a way out of the suffering that was to come, begging God to "take the cup" from Him (Luke 22:42). But unlike Abraham's story, God did not provide an alternative sacrifice. Jesus cried out from the cross, saying, "My God, my God, why have you forsaken me?" Yet no voice came from heaven. This time, the Son died.

Faith is being sure of what we hope for and certain of what we do not see.

During this dark time, it did not make sense for Jesus to obey His Father. Surely, there was a better way to carry out God's plan. Nevertheless, Jesus trusted His Father and demonstrated for us an unprecedented faithfulness. As Paul notes in his writings, this kind of faith leads to a right relationship with God. Trusting God is a way of life for believers, because they "live by faith" (Romans 1:17; 2 Corinthians 5:7; Galatians 2:20; 3:11). But, like with the case of Jesus, carrying our own crosses sometimes does not make sense. It is a hard, impractical route to take, leaving us gasping for breath. There must be a better way, we rationalize. Surely God does not require this kind of faithfulness from us. But, from the example of Jesus, we press on in the face of uncertainty. We press on although we don't "feel" like it. We trust that, like with the examples of Abraham and Jesus, God will come through with His promises, even if it is not until the third day.

Reflect on this...

What are some ways that God has proved His faithfulness to you in the past? How might these aid you in trusting God in the future?

Reflect on an area of your life where you need to put your faith in God. Resolve to be steadfast to Him even though you may not see immediate results.

NOTES:

7

Self-control

Self-control as a fruit of the Spirit is probably one of the most difficult for us to understand. The term itself begins with "self" and that would appear to be opposite of being spirit-controlled. So what is it doing on Paul's list of the fruit of the Spirit? What is the value of this fruit for the Christian?

Self-control *(enkrateia)* is unique in the list since it is not found in the Old Testament and only comes into the Jewish literature during the Hellenistic period with Philo, the Essenes and inter-testamental writings. However, we should not take this to mean that it is not an important fruit of the Spirit. In Greek grammar, the words which come first and last in a list are usually the most important. Love (*agapē*) is the first on the list and no one would argue against its importance. And self-control is the very last word after which Paul says, "Against such things there is no law" (Galatians 5:23). Although this translation has this last clause as a separate sentence, Greek scholars usually include it as part of the sentence which begins, "But the fruit of the Spirit is love . . ." (Galatians 5:22). Paul had good reason to put self-control right before he makes a statement about the law.

Much of Roman thought and law came from the Greeks and this first century was part of what is called the Hellenistic period. Even today the Greek name for Greece is Elláda, or officially as the Hellenic Republic. Socrates, a famous Greek philosopher whose ideas come to us primarily through the writings of Plato (since Socrates did not write anything down), viewed *enkrateia* (self-control) as a "cardinal virtue." For the Stoic school of philosophy *enkrateia* was very important carrying the meaning of relating to "people who freely control all things, maintaining freedom in self-restraint."[20] Since Stoicism was the most prominent philosophy of the first century AD it is important that we unpack what it meant in the first century for the average person.

The primary meaning of this word for the Stoics was self-control in matters of sex.[21] If one could control oneself sexually, then one could certainly control the other human drives and tendencies! The human goal for these first century people was to find a balance in life, a harmony with their environment. The Stoics believed in fatalism, where people could not control what happens to them, but they could control their own attitudes and make choices in behavior that would make their lives more consistent and balanced. The Jewish philosopher, Philo, was strongly influenced by Hellenistic ideas and held self-control in high regard as "superiority expressed in self-restraint."[22] This implies that the people with self-control have the power to do more than they chose to do. So Paul saw the Galatians as people who have relative freedom and autonomy. Their lives are not tightly controlled by outside forces. They have choices!

Reflect on this...

Would you place self-control as the second most important fruit of the Spirit as Paul does? Why or why not?

What aspects of our contemporary society make self-control significant for the Christian? Why?

Would you agree that the sex drive is the most difficult human drive to control as the first century people seemed to believe? Why or why not?

Self-control is not found at all in the Gospels, however, a synonym (*sōphrōsynē*, sober or sane) is used in Mark 5:15 and Luke 8:35 in describing the result of Jesus healing the demon-possessed man in the region of the Gerasenes. This was a person who previously no person or chains could restrain. But after his healing, he was "dressed and in his right mind." "In his right mind" is how this synonym is translated, emphasizing that his ability to control himself is considered something a sane person can do.

Sobriety or sanity was considered more important than *enkrateia* in the works of the Stoic philosophers. In popular Stoic lists of virtues in the first century it is a virtue of rulers, professional people, and women.[23] Classical scholars tell us that it has central significance for "an aristocratic mode of life" and that for Aristotle it is the response of a wise person who has the power to do whatever he wants, but choses restraint over stupidity.[24] Many Stoic philosophers came from the upper classes, were well-educated and thus became the spokespersons through their writings.

In some contexts it is translated as "chastity." This goes back again to the idea of control of the sexual appetites, just like *enkrateia*. Women, especially, were taught to be chaste as their illicit sexual behavior would bring shame on the families they belonged to. Perhaps Paul did not use this synonym because of its association with rulers and the aristocracy. His audience more likely identified with the lower classes.

Our term, *enkrateia* (self-control) is found once in Acts 24:25, twice in 2 Peter 1:6 and the other five times in Paul's letters. The Acts occurrence is during Paul's defense before the Roman governor, Felix and his wife Drusilla (a Jewess). Paul's dialogue with Felix about righteousness, self-control and coming judgment startled Felix. He asked Paul to leave him and he would call for him at some other time. Perhaps an ancient instance of "Don't call me, I'll call you!"

Reflect on this...

Do you see self-control as a virtue which is needed by the wealthy or more powerful in society more than by the poor or oppressed? Why or why not?

Do you see "sanity" and self-control as synonyms today? Why or why not?

In our holiness tradition, much emphasis has been placed on what a holy person does not do. Growing up, I learned that a holy person did not dance, smoke, drink, "do drugs" or associate with people who do these things. And though, I suppose, one could say that I exercised "self-control" in not doing these things, they were really not even temptations for me. In classes, I did associate with people at the public high school who were tempted and did participate in these behaviors. But for the most part, I lived in a community where I didn't encounter those who could entice me to do these things. I had a very strong relationship with my Christian parents and siblings and my social life revolved around the church youth activities.

My understanding of self-control as a young person came more in the areas of time management, over-commitment, eating, and sleeping. There was nothing inherently wrong with the use of my time, my energy, what I ate or how much I slept. But these things which I did have some measure of control over, needed to be guided and directed by the Holy Spirit! The story of creation tells us that God created all and it was good. So it is not so much the issue that we are to avoid "bad" things, but that we are to use God's creation in the way that it was intended to be used.

The Christian understanding of self-control is that we allow the Holy Spirit to live and act through us.

This particular fruit of the Spirit needs to be understood for what it is—a fruit of the Spirit. It is not "a clenching our teeth—I'm going to do this or die trying" kind of activity which depends solely on our own human strength. Christians do not believe in autonomous self-mastery,[25] but we do believe that God can guide and direct our behavior to honor Him as we allow His Holy Spirit to work in our lives. That doesn't mean we will always do the right thing, but it does mean that the Holy Spirit will be faithful to correct us when we do swerve from God's will for our lives.

When we become aware of the fact that we have missed the mark of pleasing God, we ask for forgiveness and our relationship with God is healed and strengthened. This is the process of growing in grace. This is the work of holiness in our lives. There is nothing we can do to earn our salvation, even though "not doing certain things" or exercising self-control is often a temptation for Christians to substitute for a vital and growing relationship with the God of creation! The Christian understanding of self-control is that we allow the Holy Spirit to live and act through us, which then brings us back to the first fruit of the Spirit—love!

Reflect on this...

What issues, relationships, or situations in your life need you to exercise self-control? Why?

Do you agree that there are no "bad" created things in this world—just things that are not used as God intended? Why?

*In what ways is self-control an expression of God's love ("**agapē**")?*

NOTES:

Notes

1. Gerhard Kittel, *Theological Dictionary of the New Testament*, Vol. 1 (Grand Rapids, MI: Wm. B. Eerdmans Publishing Company, 1964), p. 35

2. Kittel, Vol. 1, p. 37

3. C. S. Lewis, *Letters to Malcolm, Chiefly on Prayer.* New York: Harcourt, Brace & World, 1964, p. 93.

4. Lyons, p. 349.

5. "Joy." *Dictionary of Biblical Imagery.* Eds. Leland Ryken, James C. Wilhoit, and Tremper Longman III. Downers Grove, IL: InterVarsity Press, 1998.

6. Lyons, p. 350.

7. Buechner, Frederick. *Now and Then: A Memoir of Vocation.* New York: HarperOne, 1991, p. 73.

8. Kittel, Vol. IV, p. 375.

9. Lyons, p. 351.

10. Kittel, Vol. I, p. 11.

11. See Bruce Malina, *The New Testament World: Insights from Cultural Anthropology (*Atlanta, GA: John Knox Press, 1981), pp. 29-33.

12. Gerhard Friedrich, Ed. *Theological Dictionary of the New Testament,* Vol. IX (Grand Rapids, MI: Wm. B. Eerdmans Publishing Company, 1974), pp. 485.

13. Friedrich, Vol. IX, p. 485.

14. Friedrich, Vol. IX, pp. 483-492.

15. Walter Bauer, William F. Arndt and F. Wilbur Gingrich, A *Greek-English Lexicon of the New Testament and Other Early Christian Literature* (Chicago: University of Chicago Press, 1957), p. 894.

16. Friedrich, Vol. VI, pp.646

17. Friedrich, Vol. VI, pp. 647-648

18. "Faith." *New Interpreter's Dictionary of the Bible: D-H.* Volume 2. Nashville: Abingdon Press, 2007.

19. Madeleine L'Engle. *Walking on Water.* New York: North Point Press, 1980.

20. Kittel, Vol. II, p. 341

21. Bauer, Arndt and Gingrich, p. 215.

22. Kittel, Vol. II, p. 341

23. Friedrich, Vol. VII, p. 1100

24. Friedrich, Vol. VII, p. 1099

25. Kittel, Vol II, p. 342

Other Dialog studies also available!

EVERYDAY CHRISTIAN

Living Like Christ Seven Days a Week

What does it mean to be a Christian outside the four walls of the church? *Everyday Christian* will help you understand how being a Christian impacts your home, work, play, environment, health, and community.

PARTICIPANT'S GUIDE ISBN: 978-0-8341- 3098-2
FACILITATOR'S GUIDE ISBN: 978-0-8341-3097-5

THE SOWER WENT OUT

And Other Parables of Jesus

With a fresh and relevant perspective, this book examines the messages of the parables of *The Sower, The Good Samaritan, The Prodigal Son, The Pharisee and Publican, The Wise and Foolish Builder, The Workers in the Vineyard,* and *The Ten Virgins.*

PARTICIPANT'S GUIDE ISBN: 978-0-8341-3102-6
FACILITATOR'S GUIDE ISBN: 978-0-8341-3101-9

Available online at DialogSeries.com